God Particles

Also by Thomas Lux

Memory's Handgrenade, 1972

The Glassblower's Breath, 1976

Sunday, 1979

Half Promised Land, 1986

The Drowned River, 1990

Split Horizon, 1994

The Blind Swimmer: Selected Early Poems, 1970–1975, 1996

New and Selected Poems, 1975–1995, 1997

The Street of Clocks, 2001

The Cradle Place, 2004

God Particles

Thomas Lux

Houghton Mifflin Company
Boston New York 2008

www.houghtonmifflinbooks.com

Library of Congress Cataloging-in-Publication Data
Lux, Thomas, date.
God particles / Thomas Lux.
p. cm.
ISBN-13: 978-0-618-93182-8
ISBN-10: 0-618-93182-1
I. Title.
PS3562.U87G63 2008
811'.54—dc22
2007038414

Printed in the United States of America

Book design by Lisa Diercks
Typeset in Whitman

WOZ 10 9 8 7 6 5 4 3 2 1

Many of the poems in this book first appeared in the following publications: *American Poetry Review:* The Happy Majority, The Joy-Bringer, The Gentleman Who Spoke Like Music, The Shooting Zoo, The Utopian Wars, And the Mice Made Marriage All Night, Sex After Funerals, Why. *Atlanta Journal-Constitution:* A Clearing, a Meadow, in Deep Forest. *Chattahoochee Review:* Jesus' Baby Teeth, The Deathwatch Beetle, Vinegar on Chalk, Cliffs Shining with Rain. *Coal Hill Review:* The American Duel. *Cooweescowee Review:* Midmorning. *Five Points:* Sleep's Ambulance, Eyes Scooped Out and Replaced by Hot Coals, Toad on Golf Tee, Her Hat, That Party on Her Head, The Pier Aspiring. *Fling:* The Grand Climacteric. *Georgia Review:* The Ambrosiana Library. *Inkwell:* Early Blur. *Knockout:* Apology to My Neighbors for Beheading Their Duck, The Lead Hour, Lump of Sugar on an Anthill, Puzzlehead. *Lumina:* Man Pedaling Next to His Bicycle. *Margie:* Their Feet Shall Slide in Due Time. *St. Petersburg Review:* Gravy Boat Goes over Waterfall. *Swink:* Behind the Horseman Sits Black Care. *Terminus:* Stink Eye, God Particles, Mole Emerging from Trench Wall, Verdun, 1916, The Harmonic Scalpel, Sugar Spoon. *Third Coast: Nolens Volens* (Whether Willing or Unwilling), Autobiographophobia. *TriQuarterly:* The Republic of Anesthesia. *Verb:* Hitler's Slippers, The Hungry Gap-Time. *Willow Springs:* Blue Vistas Glued, The First Song, How Difficult, Peacocks in Twilight.

For

Peter Davison, Alice Stone Ilchman,

Judith Moore, and James Randall

in memoriam and in gratitude

"Oh, to vex me, contraries meet in one."

—John Donne

"I do not remember our friend's name, but he was a good man."

—Ralph Waldo Emerson, on leaving
Henry Wadsworth Longfellow's funeral

Contents

I

The Gentleman Who Spoke Like Music 3
Behind the Horseman Sits Black Care 4
The Hungry Gap-Time 5
Hitler's Slippers 6
Sleep's Ambulance 7
Lump of Sugar on an Anthill 8
Stink Eye 9
The Lead Hour 10
The First Song 11
Peacocks in Twilight 12
Nolens Volens (Whether Willing or Unwilling) 13
Gravy Boat Goes over Waterfall 14
The General Law of Oblivion 15
Midmorning 16
Put the Bandage on the Sword and Not the Wound 17
The Harmonic Scalpel 18
The Republic of Anesthesia 19
Man Pedaling Next to His Bicycle 20
Her Hat, That Party on Her Head 21
Eyes Scooped Out and Replaced by Hot Coals 22
The Pier Aspiring 23

II

God Particles 27
Their Feet Shall Slide in Due Time 28
Invective 29
Jesus' Baby Teeth 30
How Difficult 31
Apology to My Neighbors for Beheading Their Duck 32
Antinomianism 33
5,495 34
The Utopian Wars 36
The Joy-Bringer 37

III

The Happy Majority   41

Cliffs Shining with Rain   42

The Shooting Zoo   43

The Ambrosiana Library   44

The Deathwatch Beetle   46

Mole Emerging from Trench Wall, Verdun, 1916   47

The Grand Climacteric   48

Vaticide   49

Early Blur   50

Sex After Funerals   51

Puzzlehead   52

Blue Vistas Glued   53

The American Duel   54

Toad on Golf Tee   55

And the Mice Made Marriage All Night   56

Vinegar on Chalk   57

Autobiographophobia   58

Sugar Spoon   60

A Clearing, a Meadow, in Deep Forest   61

NOTES   63

I

The Gentleman Who Spoke Like Music

—for Peter Davison, 1928–2004

was kind to me
though he did not have to be.
Who brought into the world a thousand books.
(Right there: a life well lived.)
Who wrote a dozen or so himself,
some prose about others,
some his own poems.
(Right there: a life lived well!)
Who corrected my spelling, gently, and
my history too, who once
or twice a year
would buy me lunch
and later let me leave his office
with shopping bags of books to read.
Who wore a bowtie sometimes,
and a vest, I think even a hanky
in his jacket pocket.
Who was generous to me,
the gentleman who spoke like music, who
was kind to me
though he did not have to be.

Behind the Horseman Sits Black Care,

and behind Black Care sits Slit Throat with a whip,
and on Slit Throat's shoulders, heels in his ribs,
there, there rides Nipple Cancer, and on her back
rides Thumbscrew. No one rides Thumbscrew's shoulders.
Certain suicide, everyone knows not to try that,
everyone, that is, who wants to get older.
Even Pee Stain, the kid whose lunch money,
instead of being stolen,
he's forced to swallow,
even Pee Stain
knows not to ride Thumbscrew's shoulders.
The Horseman (and, presumably,
his horse) prefers none
of this — Black Care with his arms
around his waist as if he's his girlfriend
and those others stacked atop him
like a troupe of acrobats, unbalanced.
The Horseman desires a doorway,
a cave's mouth, a clothesline — or best: a low, hard,
garrotey branch.

The Hungry Gap-Time,

late August, before the harvest, every one of us worn down
by the plow, the hoe, rake,
and worry over rain.
Chicken coop confiscated
by the rats and the raptors
with nary a mouse to hunt. The corn's too green and hard,
and the larder's down
to dried apples
and double-corned cod. We lie on our backs
and stare at the blue;
our work is done, our bellies flat.
The mold on the wheat killed hardly a sheaf.
The lambs fatten on the grass, our pigs we set
to forage on their own—they'll be back
when they whiff the first shucked ears
of corn. Albert's counting
bushels in his head
to see if there's enough to ask Harriet's father
for her hand. Harriet's father
is thinking about Harriet's mother's bread
pudding. The boys and girls
splash in the creek,
which is low but cold. Soon, soon
there will be food
again, and from what our hands have done
we shall live another year here
by the river
in the valley
above the fault line
beneath the mountain.

Hitler's Slippers

were hand embroidered, first with a round, red
rising sun, upon which, centered,
was sewn the symbol—who would bow
for long to such a crippled
wheel?—by which his reign is known.
Hitler's slippers were a gift
(someone else opened the package for him) from a mother,
grandmother, who bent over them for months.
She knew no other way to serve him, therefore, stitch
by stitch she adorned his slippers,
two-thirds of the Axis
represented (*ciao* Italy already)
to please the leader's eyes when he slung
his legs out of bed in the bunker
to begin another day with dry toast,
milk, and one egg, poached.

Sleep's Ambulance

takes me to a quiet room down the long hallway, into the golden elevator,
which *whooshes* me beneath—the wheat fields are stripped
but the hay fields green—down to the many streams, estuaries
like the veins on the back of a hand, flowing to the fingers' tips
and draining into the air beyond.
Did someone turn a soothing siren on?
I think I hear a siren. The factory whistle—Father's home
for supper before the evening shift? It's something of a squeaky song.
Happy little mice, I think, eating through a sack of bones.

Lump of Sugar on an Anthill

The dumb ants hack and gnaw it off grain by grain
and haul it down to the chamber
where they keep such things
to feed their queen and young. The smart ants
dig another entrance, wait for rain.
Which melts the sugar,
and through viaducts they direct it
to their nurseries, the old ants' home, the unantennaed ward,
and so on — the good little engineering ants!
The dumb ants have to eat their sugar dry.
Put your ear to a dumb ant's anthill's hole — mandibles on
sandpaper is what you'll hear.
The dumb ants pray it doesn't rain *before*
they've done their task,
or else they will drown — in sweetness,
but drown, nonetheless.

Stink Eye:

what the mongoose gives the cobra. The eye
that says: be confident
with your poison while
I kill you with *my* teeth — nonvenomous,
nor as sharp. Stink
Eye: the slit-eyes of a boy
on the trolley from Tijuana
to San Diego, late, telling me: where you get off,
I get off and rob you. Stink Eye: mine,
saying to him, Good luck, *fututor matris,*
which means motherfucker
in Latin. My whole life I've been an educator;
the children come to me
to learn their ABCs.
Stink Eye: the broken, bitter eye
of spite — keep that eye from me, and
furthermore, Lordy, Lordy,
keep me from wearing that eye,
which looks outward and leaks inward,
eating first the brain
on its way to eating the heart.
Only these things: blindfolds, clouds
of cataracts, sharp sticks,
eyewash of acid, lids sewn
shut, lids sewn open
facing nuclear blast, every boy armed
with a BB gun — only these,
and one more hope as recourse
against Stink Eye: hold
the gray backside of a mirror
to your face and return it
to its sender.

The Lead Hour

A block of black salt sits
on his chest and on that
a block, a city block, of ice.
Swallowed: one ton (metric) of metal shavings.
In his pockets: every cannonball on earth
except the ones glued in pyramids
near cannons on town hall lawns.
His wallet's solid steel, size of a toaster!
Like the men pulling the guy wires
on the *Hindenburg* just before the spark
was set: that same strength
hauling his eyelids down.
Two hours before dawn: the lead hour.
Late afternoon, winter: the lead hour.
He's got his stone visor on, stone shoes,
and granite cravat, a bag on his back
full of hammers' heads: ball-peen, claw, and sledge.
Each finger held down by staples
big as goalposts! Notwithstanding,
after all, in any event — under it,
under the lead hour,
he works.

The First Song

was sung after the first stone was thrown at a beast,
after a spear in a man's hand
brought down a pile of meat.
Of course we sang of that!
We hardly had a language and we sang.
We sang the stories, which turned into better stories,
which is why stories are told
and told again. Then, when we had more time
and bellies full enough with food,
we sang of love. But it began
with stones and sharpened sticks,
then sharpened sticks hardened
in fire.

Peacocks in Twilight

I think not, because I'll shoot both his eyes out
with one bullet. Lest you think I advocate
the blinding of peacocks in twilight,
I don't: to shoot both eyes out
shoots out, too, his frontal lobe, ergo, the bird is dead,
blind in one eye for a split second maybe, but
dead, bird brain dead. I'll do this
from the porch on a summer
evening, a pitcher of lemonade
on my left. Though I dislike doilies,
I'll place one of Mother's under
the pitcher. She insisted
on that, and my sister too. I'll use my daddy's gun.
Daddy didn't like peacocks
in twilight either, they offended
an iron aesthetic of his, something to do
with loathing cheap beauty, the meretricious,
which I must have inherited,
or else I love to hear and see
the peahens weep.

Nolens Volens (Whether Willing or Unwilling)

Whether half willing, half in love, half unwilling, half-witted
or quarter-, you will be called down to the water,
the muddy pond bank dotted
with duck drops,
the half-high river
behind a cheap motel. You will be ordered down there
to stand and stare
at the unmoved surface (*volens*, as in a pond)
or at what moves along, slowly, but: moves (*nolens*, as in a river).
You will be drawn to downward, whether alert or not,
whether glue-fingered, torn from, propelled toward, or releasing
bye-bye easily: *nolens volens*. It's a song
the girls sing jumping rope,
the boys sing as they hang from trees
by limbs, from limbs:
here's the path,
here's the hatch,
here's the catch.
Here's the *nolens*, here's the *volens*.

Gravy Boat Goes over Waterfall

Over the falls it goes, the gravy boat,
spout first. The helmsman holds on hard.
The oarsmen draw in their oars.
It's a long way down and the rocks
below rush to smack their craft
to splintereens. Two miles downriver,
at Floater's Bend, a few bodies
wash ashore (one run through
by his oar) and two survivors: a rat
in a sailor suit and the fat
lady sitting in the bow whom the captain
noticed moments before he went,
twice, down with his ship.
She was sewing, in her lap,
a tiny blue suit. Too small,
he thought, even for a doll.

The General Law of Oblivion,

Mr. Proust called it: the beloved gone so long
you forget what he/she looks like,
no matter portraits, photos, or memory,
which is the best tool for forgetting.
Though one cannot deny
its genius, Mr. Proust's prose
kills me, it loops
me over and out. Is it just French novelists
who don't know how to end
a sentence and so love the semicolon ("the period
that leaks") they can't write two lines
without one? And I am *so* godamned tired
of hearing about that cookie!
As if he were the first (first fish were!) to notice
the powers of the olfactory! But
about the General Law of Oblivion
he had it zeroed: "It breaks my heart
that I am going to forget you," he said
in a last letter to a friend.
The length and music of *that* sentence
is perfect, in English or in French.

Midmorning,

accompanied by bees
banging the screen,
blind to it between them
and the blooms
on the sill, I turn pages,
just as desperate as they
to get where I am going.
Earlier, I tried to summon
my nervous friend,
a hummingbird, with sugar
water. The ants got there first.
Now, one shrill bird
makes its noise too often,
too close: *ch-pecha, ch-pecha-pecha.*
If he'd eat the caterpillars
(in sizes S to XXL!) eating my tomatoes,
we could live as neighbors, but
why can't he keep quiet
like the spiders and snakes?
I spoke to an exterminator
once who said he'd poison
birds but he didn't want me
to write about it. I have not
until now, and now starts up
that black genius, the crow,
who is answered by the blue
bully, the ubiquitous, the utterly
American, jay.

Put the Bandage on the Sword and Not the Wound

It must hurt, too, the sword, heated to red (exactly: burnt
orange) hot, beaten and beaten, hard,
by a strong arm
and a hammer
up and down its long body, plunged
in icy water,
then beaten again
and then the grinding, the awful grinding
of stone on steel
before the thick and bitter taste of blood
on its lip.

The Harmonic Scalpel

Of all the tools a surgeon holds,
the knife that hums its way
to where the surgeon wants to go, of all the tools,
that's the best. The patient hears
the tune (the anesthesia local) and is soothed.
Sometimes a nurse (oh white
on white and her nylons too!)
will sway to it, though not
the surgeon: his or her
tapping-toe's shoe
is nailed to the floor.
The knife's a radiant singer
but the hand must be steady, still. The harmonic scalpel
sings its way to the heart,
which needs attending to.
It's red, it's blue: boom, boom, boom.
Above, in the operating theater's low-lit balcony,
the medical students,
in loose green pants
and shirts, with hands
learning to find the body's stress
on and beneath the skin,
the medical students kiss,
and, each the other, caress.

The Republic of Anesthesia

I don't feel anything today, my country-
men and -women, I'm numbed by 21 liters
of Novocain, I feel nothing
from my cowlick to the final ridge of my big toe's nail; my tear
ducts dry-walled, not a sob
or the sigh of an ant left in me this autumn,
another autumn
in which the world hates itself so much.
Man ties severed head of another man
to the tail of a dog.
One frog eats a smaller frog.
Wisdom teeth, instead of being yanked,
evolve to wisdom fangs.
All day: arid hairsplitting, cheese-paring.
One bank buys another bank
and the little rubber thimble
on the teller's thumb—that stays the same.
Certainly my god
can rip the heart from your god's chest
and will, god willing, with my help.
A trillion-milligram hammer,
the arc of its swing
wide as a ring
of Saturn, hits us first
on the right temple,
then on the left. *Good night, good night,
lights out!* bark the stars.

Man Pedaling Next to His Bicycle

—for Laure-Anne Bosselaar

Look at him go
nowhere, his feet whirring, furious. He bends forward to cut
drag, the flair
of his hat shooting the air
over it and down its back slope
for propulsion. Up hills
he's on his toes,
stands and pushes — it's slower
than usual going nowhere next to his sleek, ultralight,
green racer, which is upright,
kickstand unemployed; unridden.
Ring-ring, goes my bell, he says.
Fly in the wind, handlebars' white streamers, he says.
Flapflapflapflapflap goes the ace
of spades in the spokes.
When the road turns downhill he pedals *ahead*
of his bicycle until it catches him,
but never passes him, at the bottom
which opens to the salt flats, the listless,
grayish-white rest of the ride,
the long, level, parching road.
He pedals
beside his bicycle, pedals
and pedals,
wondering where the mountains went,
the pastures, swing sets, the humans tending
to human things. Where did they
go — that which, those whom, he was meant to glide past,
or love, on his journey?

Her Hat, That Party on Her Head

I saw first, and only, her hat. I saw neither face nor shoulder.
No lawn or garden nearby.
No white tablecloths, champagne flutes,
or trays of treats pierced by toothpicks
that fit
with her hat
at this place: a side street in a village in a country
across a border. Looking, with bad directions,
for a bus, brought me here.
Behind a rectory, a priest, in his robe, read
a newspaper, leaning back in a chair
with his bare
feet on a table. I've never seen
such white feet!
I saw also: dust, stained laundry on lines, two roosters.
Some sagging wires hung above.
Then, on the other side of a fence, her hat rising
and dropping with each step.
She walked the fence's length and disappeared.
She returned and walked the fence again.
She was walking a circuit, pain's little looping course.
She walked slowly
and too often her head tipped forward: her eyes turned down
beneath the garden, the birthday party,
on her head. Who is gone so long from her?
Beneath the bougainvillea and lily,
beneath fuscia's little lamps,
beneath the yellows and greens and blues,
whose absence
made her wear this hat
to help, but fail, to let this absence go?

Eyes Scooped Out and Replaced by Hot Coals

The above-the-punishment, the mild-
but-just punishment, symbolic,
the great advance our planet
most needs.
The procedure is painless,
using methods currently available
only in cartoons. Polls were taken:
the results were overwhelmingly in favor.
The justness of it,
known in the bone
by each of our nation, is undeniable. Thus, it is proclaimed,
on this day *anno domino*, etc., I, the final arbiter
and ultimate enforcer
of such things (appointed by the king!), make official
and binding, this: that the eyes shall be gouged out
and replaced by hot coals
in the head, *the blockhead*,
of each citizen who,
upon reaching his/her majority,
has yet to read
Moby-Dick, by Mr. Herman Melville (1819–1891), American novelist
and poet.

The Pier Aspiring

See if you can see how far out it goes. See? You can't see the end!
I'd take you out there
but it's a six-hour walk
and the work's redundant: one board laid down after another.
When the sun is high
the boards are hot.
Splinters always pose a problem walking any other way but straight.
What keeps me working on it, driving piles,
hauling timber, what's kept my hand
on the hammer, the barnacle scraper,
what keeps me working through the thirst,
the nights when the waves' tops pound
the pier from beneath, what keeps me glad
for the work, the theory is, despite the ridicule
at the lumberyard, the treks with pails
of nails (my arms
two centimeters longer each trip), the theory
is this: it's my body's habit,
hand over foot, paycheck to paycheck,
it's in the grain of my bones,
lunch bucket to lunch box.
It's good to wear an X
on my back, to bend my back to the sky, it's right
to use the hammer and the saw,
it's good to sleep
out there — attached at one distant end
and tomorrow adding to that distance.
The theory
is: It will be a bridge.

II

God Particles

God explodes, supernovas, and down upon the whole planet
a tender rain of Him falls
on every cow, ladle, leaf, human, ax handle, swing set.
We rush from our houses,
farmers standing, saved, in the rain after years of drouth.
Like snowflakes, each God particle is different,
though unlike snowflakes,
are warm and do not melt
but are absorbed by the skin.
Every human, every creature, rock, tomato on earth
is absorbing God!
Who just asked: Why did God explode?
And why ask this far into the story?
I believe He did it to Himself: *nobody*
walks into God's house, His *real* house, on a hill
in Beulah Land, *nobody*
walks into His house wearing a suicide belt.
No plane flies high enough to drop a bomb on His house.
No one will trespass
to plant an IED in His driveway.
Why did God do it?
Guilt because He sent His son
to do a job He should have done Himself?
I don't think so. God knows,
there's no reason for God to feel guilt.
I think He was downhearted, weary, too weary
to be angry anymore, or vengeful,
or even forgiving, and He wanted each of us,
and all the things we touch
and are touched by,
to have a tiny piece of Him,
though we are unqualified
for even the crumb of a crumb.

Their Feet Shall Slide in Due Time

Hard, balanced in their stance, the truth setting the eye
to the rifle scope's crosshairs, where X,
where all evil, lies.
Steady the hand,
pull back the pointing finger (*squeeeeze,*
don't jerk, the trigger, each century's
manual says). A man's a problem? Kill
the man. Problem's gone. Stalin said something like that,
or was it Gandhi? Deuteronomy
says, in a book of metaphors, sooner
or later the wicked, the venal,
shall face a steep, greasy hill whose fortress
they cannot take. Their feet shall slide
sooner or later: the fall, the reward, uh-huh, the fiery lake,
or the happy place.

Invective

Boils, pocks, and blood blisters, I pray you suffer them,
your goat grow fevered
and leak the yellow milk, I pray moles claw holes
in your head, stones be always in your shoe, fire
in your neck, slop in your cooking pot.
I pray there be rubber bullets in your gun,
I pray your daughter marry for love,
I pray your son wish to be a poet.
I pray your mother take a young lover in front of your father,
I pray it be revealed you keep your toothpicks in your beard,
I pray you be turned down
if you register to vote, I pray your wife fucks you
in the ass, I pray all your lug-nut-dumb offscourings
disdain you, I pray your next breath,
and each one thereafter, fills your lungs
with the stink of your corpse.

Jesus' Baby Teeth

for sale: left front canine (C), two upper
right molars (I, J), and his two front teeth (E, F),
which were all he wanted
for Christmas. Stains,
wear patterns on molars indicate a diet
of fish, coarse bread, and watery wine.
Also for sale: the right forefinger
of Saint Thomas, the one that plugged the hole
in Jesus' side, which action was wasted because
he didn't die (or, he *did* die
but then arose,
which is enough like not dying
to *be* not dying!) anyway. Also
a swatch of blue from the sleeve
of Mary's robe where you-know-who
laid his downy head. We're also offering
a piece (6" x 8") of the True Cross, which is signed
by the other Mary,
the one we love less
for her heart of gold.
Click on thumbnails for pictures of Jesus' left thumbnail, lost in an accident
by hammer, on the job.
Its bright moon is half risen above the horizon
but not one star
in its cracked, blackened sky.

How Difficult

for the quadriplegics to watch
the paraplegics play.
How difficult the day
the ventilator of one lung
shut down, the heart's monitor saying
ta-thump, ta-thump, ta-thump
and the screen showing *aaaaaaaaaaaa,*
and the lady down the hall
howling: *My legs are on fire! My legs are on fire!*
How difficult the icy abstract of the wintry mind.
How difficult *the cracking of houses at their ruin.*
How difficult to mow an empty grave's grass.
How difficult to ride
the landslide's lip descendingly, to endure
the day's chop-logical drip-feed of lies,
how difficult hearing
God's last scratchy — what did He say? — radio broadcast.
What did He say
about no more verbs
in the future tense?

Apology to My Neighbors for Beheading Their Duck

First, it was an accident: I did not mean
to sever his head. A book, or a being superior
or Superior, did not command it thus.
He'd gotten into the little yard we share.
He stood as still as if he were made of cement,
which, in fact, he was. Nevertheless, he was not meant
to lose his head. So that I could lop it off,
a text was not interpreted, though he was
a heterodox duck—he wore a little blue hat.
This color is proscribed for a duck's hat.
Otherwise: white duck, orange feet and beak.
A decent duck, a cause-no-trouble duck.
He weighed a hundred pounds, weighted down
your car to get him here to his new home.
Without his head, he weighs five pounds less.
Without his head, broken at the neck,
he's a less impressive duck,
but still I had no right to take it.
It belonged to him,
and he needed it, his head,
as we, as all creatures, do,
despite the swamp, the sump, thriving inside it.
He did not belong to me,
nor was he of my family.
When I dropped a bag (rather than carry it
down to the barrels beside the duck) of trash
from my fourth-floor back porch,
that's what did it, clipped it clean off,
for which I offer apologies and cash,
but I must reiterate: a book
did not tell me I had the right to do so,
nor did I hear a voice,
a promise, from a pearly place.
I did it dumb and owe you fifty bucks!

Antinomianism,

my ass!
Breaking the law of man — say, reasonable sanctions
against murder — is OK
as long a God approves it?
Problem is, which means: a man
interprets God, unpacks God's book,
a man insists
other men accept this interpretation.
This happens because
God's expository writing lacks lucidity
and He or His scribes often write sloppily.
He seems torn between tearing
out a sinner's bowels
and bestowing eyeballs
on the eyeball-less. We all know His job
is irksome, ceaseless, everybody knows
His subjects are unprincipled imbeciles,
all of His subjects this way,
all but the ones
who say God says
they are not.

5,495

times, it's said, or written (or in a movie
unseen by speaker), Jesus was whipped
on his way to Calvary. Plus, he had to carry/drag
the instrument upon which he was to be executed!
After that: no big deal, the thorny hat. Nobody should be struck
5,495 times, not Jesus, not anybody, with a whip — not in a day, a lifetime.
I wonder, though, who counted, and was a cat-o'-nine-tails
(common over eons)
one of the whips, and does it count for one lash or nine?
Did the lash-counter carry an abacus?
Nobody should be whipped 5,495 times,
not Jesus, not anybody.
Those in the tumbrel hundreds of years later
on their way to the burning stake
didn't get whipped that many times.
Sure, they were tortured beforehand
but not whipped that many times!
A Jew on the way to the gas chamber didn't (*collectively*
is another story), nor did he carry
the gas chamber on his back
to the gas chamber site. Nobody: 5,495 times! An Armenian
didn't get whipped
that many times driven on his death trek.
The men who might have been the fathers
of myself and my friends, on the Bataan death march,
didn't get whipped that many times, though rifle butts smashed into clavicles
and bullets to the cerebellum
were quotidian. I don't think
the whip was used much at Andersonville.
Slaves, of course, where whipped for thousands
of years, and since the age
of photography we have seen the welts
that even in black and white are red. But 5,495 times
in a few hours!

All those flailings
you took for us, Jesus, thank you.
The speaker blames you not
for each time you didn't show up, when a prophet said you would,
at the ongoing party
of carnage (you had no way of knowing!)
every day in your name,
and/or your father's, or
some other god's, God forgive me.

The Utopian Wars

Amish raiding party attacks a Quaker
settlement at Muddy Crossing,
murdering first the Quaker ferryman
(who is drunk, and awakens only in midstream
to find an Amish man tying an anvil to his neck)
before reaching the village
and killing dozens, quietly at first, by blade
and hatchet (hoping to blame the savages), and burning nothing
as they work their way toward the center of town. Kill on the way in, burn
on the way out. In the hills, meanwhile,
the Buddhists quick-change from bright orange
to camo robes, point their howitzers eastward
where they know the Episcopalians
milk cobras
to tip their arrows.
The Baha'i sit back and sharpen their knives and saws.
The wily Mennonites withdraw,
their leaders meeting for three days
in upstate New York,
while at the same time the few remaining Jains
turn their cheeks
to reveal slashed and bloody jaws
from the last time
they turned their cheeks.

The Joy-Bringer

breaks the light through the oak leaves at dawn.
The joy-bringer injects the red bird's red.
The joy-bringer brings the green, lets the cup runneth over
into a saucer, from which you can sip.
Gives fish the river, the river the fish.
If by two inches you avoid a piano
falling on your head
and later at the hospital fall in love with the doctor
who removes a few splinters
of ivory and black piano lacquer
from your left calf: the joy-bringer
arranged that. Also the chilled artesian water
spilling from a pipe only two inches above the ground,
from which you drank on your hands and knees,
on a few boards or branches, you bowed in the muck and drank
that sweet cold reaching-up,
you drank among the skunk cabbage, ferns, a small brook
at your back: again, guess what,
the joy-bringer! In fact, let us praise
the joy-bringer for these seven
things: 1) right lung, 2) left lung, 3) heart, 4) left brain,
5) right brain, 6) tongue, 7) the body to put them in.
Thank you, joy-bringer!
And thanky, thanky too for just-mown hay
cut an inch from its roots
to bleed its perfume into the air!

III

The Happy Majority

... before I join the great and, I believe, the happy majority.
    —P. T. Barnum

Before *I* join the happy majority (though I doubt one member happy
or unhappy) I have some plans: to discover several new species
of beetle; to jump from a 100-foot platform
into a pile — big enough
to break my fall — of multicolored lingerie;
to build a little heater
(*oh not to join the happy ones*
until some tasks are done)
beside each tulip bulb to speed its bloom;
to read 42,007 books (list available
on request); to learn to read and/or write
Chinese, CAT scans, Sanskrit, petroglyphs,
and English; to catch a bigot
(*oh not to join the happy ones*
until some tasks are done)
by the toe; to kiss
the clavicle of (name available
on request); to pay my respects, again,
at the grave of John Keats; to abrogate
my position in God's nihilistic
(*oh not to join the happy ones*
until some tasks are done)
dream; to hold my mother's hand as she leaves this world;
to lay my hand upon my father's heart as he does likewise;
and for my daughter to be glad I was her father as I exit, also
(in a hundred years or so), from the conscious to the un-.

Cliffs Shining with Rain

'Tis double death to drown in ken of shore.
—W. S.

Why, in a sea storm, though near shore, on a ship shipping water,
the mast cracked, why don't
sailors happily wreck
on the beach, or even
upon the rocks,
and then swim—or wade—the few yards to shore,
where one cannot drown?
They want to sail home, certainly, not lose their cargo, sail home,
not be marooned.
No shore but their own will do.
So all night they bail by bucket
and pump, all hands, all night,
because they know what I never
will, I who can fear
though not imagine
drowning, I with no cargo
to lose, and who's never sailed under wind
from a wharf where my mother
or wife or child stood. They know, the sailors know,
in a mast-snapping storm, no matter how close to shore, they know
that the waves and splintered timber, thrown
against rocks, or reef, or even beach, drawn back and dashed again,
are a bigger risk
than bailing, bailing, throwing goats, anvils, horses overboard, in order to
stand offshore, a mile or two, safe,
in deep water until,
at dawn, the wind swallows itself
and there they are, the broken cliffs,
shining with rain.

The Shooting Zoo

The giraffe can't stand up anymore: he's still tall
but not tall enough. The silverback is bald,
the zebra's black stripes gray. There's a virus at the zoo: the spring-
bok can't prong,
the alligators wracked by cataracts,
the last lion meowls like an auntie's cat.
The penguins walk as if they have a load in their pants!
The vultures are eating sandwiches and plants!
Something's wrong with all the animals: the pandas obstreperous,
the iguanas demand bananas, the loons
are out of tune.
What to do, what to do? Soon,
whatever it is that's deranging them
will pass through their bars,
across their moats,
and then: our dogs and gold-
fish, the little parakeet
who pecks our lips
so we may say it kisses us, soon
they'll start dropping too.
Next: our children? grandma?
The zookeepers don't know what to do, so
print some permits permitting men
to bring their guns to the shooting zoo.

The Ambrosiana Library

On its onyx shelves: every book you've ever read,
and the tone you felt, which pierced you,
when you did. Even those
you've forgotten
you've read. It offers all the books you want to read,
and all the books you don't know you want to read because you've never
read about them in your reading. It holds, also,
those as yet unwritten. The Ambrosiana Library
is comprehensive: every book ever written on monkeys, a mile or two, all
told, of shelves. Also: every truthful book written
by the monkeys' cousins, some several yards of these
on special shelves, more like cradles, or thrones.
Every book on joy: TAL's got it!
Every book on bananas!
The Ambrosiana Library
has long, deep-polished oak tables, green lampshades,
cream-cushioned chairs
(with, for anyone planning to read
more than three hours, magic fingers), leather armrests (for those
who read with chin in hands),
magazines in 11,000 languages,
every obscure, passionate poetry journal,
every book on everything we don't want to know
but should. The lights hanging
from oak beams above the readers
light *and* illuminate every page. Each book dusted
each day. Original jackets, no odious numbers glued to spines,
not one decimal, Dewey or otherwise, in the entire place!
Each reader is assigned
his or her personal librarian,
and each librarian is paid twice the average income
of orthopedic surgeons
and gets free orthopedic surgery

for any Ambrosiana-related (shelving
or unshelving) injury.
Mornings, whole afternoons,
citizens sit and read themselves into another
world—from which they will
return. When it's time for lunch, or to close, a tiny bell
is wrung which only humans,
not dogs, can hear. And, *and,* at the door as you leave
is a character you loved—fictional, historical, half
of each—from whatever book you're reading now
or from any book read
previously. This character (never
the writer of the book, though there are slips
of paper with the words *thank you*
on them released monthly
to the wind from a skylight
in the library's attic), this character
stands by the door to say goodbye, come again: tip of his hat,
a smile from her.
No books ever leave Ambrosiana.
It's a library you enter like a book,
and when you leave
the book leaves inside you.

The Deathwatch Beetle

surveils from his place on the window's upper ledge
beside my mother's bed—she's shaking hard,
who worked so hard, and *will not be a burden*
though she always carried one
(or two, or three) and never complained of such.
The Deathwatch Beetle is her sentinel.
His antennae twitch
as he does what he was named for, probably
by a New Englander, like her,
of English and Czech stock, like her,
who makes a stoic seem like a movie star
at a spa
recovering from a hangnail.
Let the Deathwatch Beetle
monitor my mother's death.
I shall monitor my mother's life.
I shall honor my mother's life.
She seems to be letting go
but then: *Not yet, Death,* she says,
not yet, your bug
on the sill will be a husk
before I am.

Mole Emerging from Trench Wall, Verdun, 1916

Doing his job, the mole, disturbed no doubt by the shaking
and noisy dirt, but still digging blind,
goes on with the only life he knows.
He's down there why? Eating worms? Roots?
Having his mole-being, his mole-ness?
So, doing his job, he digs, and emerges,
his head and shoulders, from the rear wall of a trench.
Maybe he was heading for Germany, therefore
it's a French trench. Or,
equally likely, he was heading toward France
and poking through the rear
of a German trench.
Moles live in most dirt in most places.
Some moles have noses shaped like stars.
This one does not.
He's a regular mole, a clock-puncher
mole: wake up, dig, eat, sleep, wake up . . .
This mole emerges,
blinking. Sergeant Falkenhayn sees him,
or Corporal Chrétien.
The mole sees little
because he does not need to in his dark.
Sergeant Falkenhayn
or Corporal Chrétien, one of them,
pinches the mole's shoulders,
softly, between his thumb
and forefinger,
pulls the whole six inches of him free,
turns him around,
puts him back, nose first, in his tunnel,
and lights a match,
which he then turns to the mole's stubby, muscular tail.

The Grand Climacteric

Stonk, stonk, stonk — mortar rounds slide
down tubes and then fly skyward
until they reach their arcs', their parabolas', peaks
(there, for a second's fraction,
they neither fall nor rise) and hang
there until . . . what makes them shatter
to white-hot shrap is: explosives,
love of death (which one cannot love
when dead), or a deep, creaking mineshaft
into which so many blind miners go
to find neither gold nor coal
and never ascend again to the surface. Sorry
to say: *Stonk, stonk, stonk, stonk.*

Vaticide,

i.e., the murder (metaphorical) of poets,
is not such a bad idea in some cases:
the case of the poet who put fish poison in her poems,
the case of the poet who put his life,
every part of it, over
and over again, in his poems.
The poet who places his poems above his mother, or child.
The poet who praises flowers in window boxes
affixed to windowless
crematoria, the poet whose poems
provide rations of sand.
Banishment would do for the poet who sleeps too little.
Banishment for the poet of pulselessness.
A slap on the bum for the poet of iron words.
A kick in the pants for nature poets who exclude worms.
A gentle dope-slap to the effete aesthetes.
And country club memberships
(including toe massages)
for all the rest
who can be gathered to the breast.

Early Blur

occurs, I say to Mary, when we catch the outline
of something and think we know it
and then we fill in the parts we don't see
with hope. I say this
to Mary, Mary of the late slant light of autumn,
Mary by the lake of wolverines,
Mary by the lake beneath which drowned a wall,
Mary of the first snow, I say to Mary,
I say: I am the river
and you are its blue, burning current.

Sex After Funerals

Hesiod (author of *Works and Days,* a solid
book title) advised against it — counterintuitive, you'd think,
from a poet
second only to Homer, if Homer existed.
(If he didn't, second only to: so what!)
And too, Hesiod spent years in bitter
litigation with his brother
over a barren hill farm and one goat.
This advice from a poet who disliked boats.
This from a poet who couldn't play the harp!
This from a man who worshiped goddesses
but disdained women,
this from a harvester who couldn't keep his scythe sharp,
this from a man
beaten to death with a log
and tossed in the sea,
and whose murderers were ID'ed
(humans refused) by his dog.

Puzzlehead

His thoughts like a deck of cards hit
by a howitzer. As they were only pieces
of thoughts in the first place, thoughts
without a beginning, middle, or end, they are now more
torn, bits
of red and black and white. Other shards
of the puzzle
in his head: some of blue sky, others a treetop, another one
a bird's foot, yellow. And piles
of gray—streaked with cream—granite. These seem
as if they belong in the same scene,
but look at this one: a loopy piece of black,
and more and more of them, all black. Half the puzzle
unbroken black!
Where does the blackness meet
the bird's foot (two toes
with visible talons), and the treetops, and what must be sky—blue,
with wisps of white?
What is the blackness thinking
about the whole mountain of blackness,
soon to rise over the afore-
mentioned granite mountain,
remedyless and truculent?

Blue Vistas Glued

How well God measures His doses! It was yesterday
the blue vistas were glued to the horizon, it was Tuesday
the pale green grasses rushed to darker green, the rivers rushed
to join another rushing — it was yesterday — river.
There were some
assuagements: the hangmen
who hanged homosexuals no longer hanged
for the same offense; more ears were sharpened,
by fear, but sharpened; there were, oh, a million kisses;
there was the child who grew to be human;
there was febrifuge, sweet febrifuge!
There was, from across the charred field,
the smell of lilacs
brought by a breeze. There were days, years,
when the clock's thinking
did not sound like: *me, me, me, me.*
There were impressive ruins.

The American Duel

Never mind the exchange of letters,
epithets, the appointing of seconds,
choosing of time and place (Vidalia,
Weehauken, The Oaks . . .),
the wrangling over the nature
of the insult ("Sir, though you may say you meant Miss Slather
no offense, your left eyebrow
indicates otherwise,
so now I must call you rude, sir, and a calumniator").
Instead of that,
let us each choose a pistol, eschew
rising early and wetting our boots
and pant cuffs with dew.
Instead, let us meet after brunch
in the undertaker's parlor,
let us sit knee to knee,
the pistol on a stool beside us.
Then, after saluting each other
and instructing our friends
our honor is ours only, let us,
let us flip a coin
and the winner shall take up the pistol
and shoot the loser
between the eyes, or if it be over an insult (as in
this case) to the fairer sex, let the winner
shoot the loser in the heart. This
is an American duel, how we fight,
how *we* respond to nose-pulling,
unlike the foppish French
or the English, who wrap their umbrellas
so astonishingly tight.

Toad on Golf Tee

First, I sought a toad in the rubble-filled ring
of a gone silo's cement
foundation. Toads like to hide and hop
there. Once acquired,
I took him to a spot
just to the peachless peach tree's left, a slightly downsloping
patch of lawn. I teed him up, sideways.
I wanted to launch him by the ribs
toward my target: a steep barn roof
forty yards away, over a driveway,
a rock garden, over more gravel
and a short swatch of bad grass.
For this I'd use a nine iron: I needed lift,
and if the toad landed where I wanted him to land
(just short of the roof's peak),
then he would roll back down: reusable, reteeable toad.
My short game was good.
The weathervane's rooster said the wind was right.
The sound—for I kept my backswing slow
and my eye on the toad—fired
to my face: *thwuuuump!*
It was a perfect pitch shot: he dropped inches from the top,
rolled a few turns earthward,
and stopped.
It took a week
and a little rain
before his disarticulated bones
slid down the sharp slope
and landed in the little valley of stones
the rain excavates
when it falls, too, from the eaves.

And the Mice Made Marriage All Night

We heard them at night in the rafters, attic,
walls, the cupboards. Now, they did not gnaw
the peanut butter poised
to snap their necks, nor eat the oatmeal
fallen between the stove and sink,
which sustained them for many weeks.
They were gladful
and tireless. The joyous scritch of their claws
caught the cat's ear,
but she didn't stir
from her spot by the stove,
not to scratch a flea.
Good to live in that house then,
with the mice, all night, making marriage,
as did we.

Vinegar on Chalk

A stain drunk deep by its host.
A stain carried by a wind passing through Starving Dog Cyn.
A stain in the birdsong, pretty birdsong.
A stain in the pile driver driving its piles.
A stain, a perdurable stain, in the root.
A stain, the first, on Mr. Keats's hanky.
A stain of spilled ether, mudsuckers, and spider bones.
A stain stinking of a tumor removed by a rasp.
A stain of vanity, self-pity's blind cousin.
A stain in the sky. No, that's a cloud.
A stain in the light, the early morning light: vinegar on chalk.
A stain, impedimenta of stains.
A stain in the blue, in the green, in the red.
A stain of sheep staining the hillside.
A stain, a deep-dyed stain.

Autobiographophobia

I shan't tell you about switching his wooden leg
with her wooden leg, I shan't confess
my lies and the lies against me: when I said I loved X
but really loved Y
and was sleeping with Z
to injure the feelings of X
who was sleeping with Z, Y, and me.
Whether I was there or not
when the sky fell, how I learned
the cure for lesions
of the heart, if it's true
or not that I keep, in a coop
on my roof, the only two extant dodo
birds (plus one dodo egg) — my lips
are sewn shut (might as well be!) with baling wire.
I had many funny uncles.
Not one ever put his hand in my pants.
Never met a dipsomaniac
until I left home
and wandered all those years, in and out, through the lives of others.
My life is one filled with blessings.
And if I've been wronged,
then for each wrong I've been multiblessed.
Which is why
I will not confide
my serial poisoning of parakeets.
It would be fruitless
to ask me regarding my part
in the extinction of sheep.
About my childhood: not a peep.
I sold my grandmother's hearing aid,
not only for cash but also to facilitate
my screaming in her face.

I loved my grandmother,
whose husband I did not know.
Because I'm telling the truth,
there is no shame.
Because I'm telling the truth, and I'm sure
it actually happened
(I was there!), because I'm telling the truth,
it is right that I talk only of myself
and never of you, or you, and you, or you.

Sugar Spoon

Low seven digits (1,000,006, approx.), until it's almost as flimsy as tinfoil,
this spoon,
plunged into the same sugar bowl
every morning, two, three, four times — for three-quarters
of a century, longer?
At night, deep in sweetness, it rests.
And at dawn, when the battered coffee pot begins to rattle,
it's still sunk in the white grains,
while outside, snow
drifts to the eaves almost,
or in summer, the sticky sugar hardens
on it in little arctic ridges. On the handle: my father's thumbprint
exactly on top of his thumbprint, thousands and thousands . . .
Between each print of his: my mother's. It's going
a bruised green in the recesses
of its engraved (viny trees,
sheep?) handle. It cost
a few pfennig once, with its bowl.
It will serve and serve
until the bottom of its shiny curve
grows so thin
a tiny hole opens
and thenceforth it will leave a dusting of its cargo,
a trail, a grainy Milky Way,
across the maple table
from the bowl to my father's, my mother's, coffee cup.

A Clearing, a Meadow, in Deep Forest

One lies down in the meadow, one hears the insects saw and gnaw
in the grass, and above, one hears
some music from childhood, sees a barn swallow diving.
One has these thoughts,
stricken. Clouds hang above the meadow's — how did
this clearing occur? — ragged
treeline. How did it happen, its edges irregular,
not cut for a field
of even rye or oats? When one first breaks
into it, the clearing,
one thinks: not large enough for a farm,
this fodder couldn't feed four cows.
One walks halfway across
and sits down, stricken. This is the place to rest,
one thinks, in the meadow's middle,
this is the place to stop
and wait for the wind, or a star, or a vole's nose
to point one on one's way.

NOTES

"The General Law of Oblivion": quoted: Bill Knott
"Behind the Horseman Sits Black Care": Horace
"How Difficult": line eleven italics: Samuel Pepys